Knight Book of Riddles

Do you know why good bread is like the sun? Or what is hot when it's cold? Or when a cat is really a sailing boat? This book will tell you.

Hundreds of riddles about birds, animals, people, cities; riddles from 'My sister Kate' and riddles in rhyme.

How to amuse yourself and your friends!

Knight Book of Riddles

Compiled and illustrated by
Richard Gregory

KNIGHT BOOKS
Hodder & Stoughton

ISBN 0 340 20183 5
Copyright © 1976 Richard E. Gregory
First published in 1976
Second impression 1976

Printed and bound in Great Britain in Knight Books for
Hodder & Stoughton Children's Books, a division of
Hodder & Stoughton Ltd., Arlen House, Salisbury Road, Leicester,
by Richard Clay (The Chaucer Press), Ltd., Bungay, Suffolk

Contents

Foreword

Riddles have been a source of fun and puzzlement from the earliest times. One of the oldest riddles we know is the riddle of the Sphinx. The Sphinx was a fabulous monster with the head and chest of a woman, the body of a lion and the wings of a bird. Guarding the road to Thebes, it would stop travellers and ask them, 'Which animal has four legs in the morning, two legs at mid-day and three legs at evening?'

If they could not answer, the Sphinx ate the travellers. Many people died on the road to Thebes because nobody knew the answer to the riddle.

A young Greek named Oedipus swore he would get rid of the monster. He journeyed along the road to Thebes till he was stopped by the Sphinx and asked to answer the riddle.

Oedipus was a clever young man and he only had to think for a little while before he found the answer. He said, 'This is the answer to your riddle. The animal is Man. In the morning, that is when he is a baby, he crawls about on his hands and knees, and so he moves on four legs. When he grows older, in the middle of his life, he walks on two legs, and in the evening of his days, when he is an old man, he uses a stick to help him to get about. So he goes on three legs.'

The Sphinx was so angry at having its riddle solved that it threw itself in the sea and was never seen again.

Another very old riddle appears in the Bible.

A Hebrew strong man named Samson was much feared by the Philistines who were at war with Samson's people.

Samson was so strong that he was not afraid of the Philistines and even went into their country to visit his

sweetheart, Delilah. He
played many tricks on his
enemies and once he teased
them by asking them a riddle.
His riddle was, 'Out of the strong
came forth sweetness.
What was it?' Even the wisest
men of the Philistines
could not find the answer.

Samson made up this riddle
after he had come face to
face with a lion while on his way to visit Delilah. He
killed the lion with his bare hands. Later, when he was
returning home, he passed the dead lion and found that a
swarm of bees had made a hive in its body. This gave him
the idea for his riddle. The answer to which was, 'Honey
came out of the body of the lion.'

Many famous people have invented riddles, among
them was Lord Byron. Because Byron was a poet, it is
not surprising that his riddle is written in the form of a
poem. Here it is:

I'm not in earth, nor the sun, nor moon.
You may search all the sky – I'm not there.
In the morning and evening – though not in the
    noon –
You may plainly perceive me, for, like a balloon,
I am midway suspended in air.
Though disease may possess me, and sickness
    and pain,
I am never in sorrow nor gloom;
Though in wit and in wisdom I equally reign,
I'm the heart of all sin and long lived in vain;
Yet I ne'er shall be found in the tomb.

And the answer is, in case you couldn't find it yourself, the letter 'i'.

Even ministers of religion have found time to relax and enjoy the exercise of inventing riddles. A famous riddle composed many years ago by Bishop Wilberforce is still remembered today to puzzle children now as it did then. It goes like this:

I am a Treasure Chest and inside me are many things. They are (1) A box (2) Two lids (3) Two tall trees (4) Some shell fish (5) Two flat fish (6) Two young farm animals (7) Two musical instruments (8) Two steps leading to a hotel (9) Something used by a carpenter (10) A deer (11) A large number of furry animals, swift and shy (12) Weapons of war (13) A number of weather cocks (14) A fruit from the garden of Eden (15) Whips without handles (16) Two scholars (17) The top of a hill (18) Part of a bell (19) What Nebuchadnezzar might have said (20) Pros and cons (21) Dutch flowers (22) Horse measurements (23) Places of worship (24) Ten Spanish noblemen (25) An Isthmus (26) Rubbish (27) Peas and beans.

The riddle is, 'What is the Treasure Chest and what are all the things in it?'

How many did you solve?

The answer is, the Treasure Chest is your body and the things that are in it are: (1) A chest (2) Eyelids (3) Palms (4) Muscles (mussels) (5) Soles (6) Calves (7) Ear drums (8) Insteps (inn steps) (9) Nails (10) Heart (hart) (11) Hairs (hares) (12) Arms (13) Veins (vanes) (14) Adam's apple (15) Lashes (16) Pupils (17) Brow (18) Tongue (19) Eyebrows (I browse) (20) Eyes and nose (ayes and noes) (21) Two lips (tulips) (22) Hands (23) Temples (24) Tendons (ten dons) (25) Neck (26) Waist (waste) (27) Pulse.

You might think that a Member of Parliament would be too concerned with affairs of state to bother about such trivial things as riddles, but Charles James Fox, a very famous politician at the end of the eighteenth century, found time to compose this problem.

> Formed long ago, yet made today,
> Employed while others sleep;
> What few would like to give away,
> Nor any wish to keep.

Perhaps he was feeling a little tired when he wrote this for the answer to his riddle is, a bed.

In this book there are hundreds of riddles, some old, some new. Some easy, some hard. Some to make you laugh and none to make you cry. I hope you will have as much fun in reading them as I had in collecting them.

Richard E. Gregory

My favourite riddle

Everybody has a favourite riddle and this is a collection of riddles from a number of young riddle lovers. Is your favourite riddle among them?

Question If all the cars in England were painted red, what would the country then be called?

Answer A red carnation (car nation)!

Q What is small, purple and dangerous?
A A grape with a machine gun!

Q When does a pig learn to write?
A When it is turned into a pen!

Q What do you call a monkey that is covered in sugar and the white of an egg?
A A meringue-u-tang!

Q What did the painter say to the wall?
A 'One more crack and I'll plaster you!'

Q What's an easy way to catch an elephant?
A Chase him up a tree in spring and wait for the fall!

Q Although I've neither legs nor feet,
   I'm only useful when I go.
   I have no tongue but yet I tell
   What hundreds want to know.
A A clock!

Q   When Columbus first discovered
    America, where
    did he stand?
A   On his feet!

Q   Why did the baker stop
    baking doughnuts?
A   He got tired of the whole
    (hole) business!

Q   Why is an elephant big, grey and wrinkled?
A   Because if it was small, white and round, it would be
    an Aspirin!

Q   Why do I fold my money?
A   Because I find it increases (in creases)!

Q   Why are books spies?
A   Because they are always under cover!

Q   What is it which is always invisible and yet never out
    of sight?
A   The letter S!

Q   What is yellow and dangerous?
A   Shark-infested custard!

Q   Why did the boy bring an axe to school?
A   Because it was breaking-up day!

Q   Why should rivers be rich?
A   Because they have banks round them!

Q   What has a mouth larger than its head?
A   A river!

Q   Which is the laziest plant and which is the most active?

A   The creeper is the laziest plant and the running vine is the most active!

Q   If a man was born in China, educated in England and buried in America, what would he be?

A   Dead!

Q   What was purple and a conqueror?

A   Alexander the Grape!

Q   Who was the first space traveller?

A   The cow that jumped over the moon!

Q   What is black, lives in a tree and is dangerous?

A   A crow with a machine gun!

Q   What is the hardest thing to do in the world?

A   Milk arrowroot biscuits!

Q   Why did the prisoner want to catch measles?

A   So he could break out!

Q   What is the highest building in New York?

A   The library because it has so many storeys (stories)!

Q   Why do you forget a tooth that has been pulled out?

A   Because it goes out of your head!

Q   What is purple and lights up?

A   An electric grape!

Q   Which was the biggest island before Australia was discovered?

A   Australia!

Q Why did the milking stool only have three legs?
A Because the cow had the other (udder)!

Q What has a hump and lives at the North Pole?
A A camel that has lost its way!

Q Where do spirits get their mail?
A From the ghost office!

Q What goes, ha ha plonk?
A A man laughing his head off!

Q What man has eyes at the back of his head?
A The man whose hindsight is better than his foresight!

Q What happens if you swallow yeast and shoe polish?
A You rise and shine!

Q When is an operation funny?
A When it leaves the patient in stitches!

Q What is the best thing to take when you are run down?
A The number of the car that hit you!

Q If you put a baby goat in a cement mixer, what would you get?
A A crazy, mixed up kid!

Q What great change takes place when wheat becomes flour?
A A change in price!

Q   What is a mini-miner?
A   A pigmy gold digger!

Q   Why is a cricket score like fried fish?
A   They both depend on the batter!

Q   Why should you not doze on trains?
A   Because trains run over sleepers!
Q   How did the blind carpenter regain his sight?
A   He picked up the hammer and saw!

Q   What kind of shoes are made from banana skins?
A   Slippers!

Q   Why do they say amen and not awoman in church?
A   Because they sings hymns (hims) not hers!

Q   What is the difference between a mouse and a pretty
    girl?
A   One harms cheese and the other charms hes!

Q   How strong is a policeman?
A   Strong enough to hold up the traffic with one hand!

Q   What did the grape say when the elephant sat on
    him?
A   Nothing, it just gave a little whine (wine)!

Q   What do you call a man who steals ham?
A   A hamburglar!

Q   What is the difference between a loving husband and
    a jilted sailor?
A   One kisses the missus and the other misses the
    kisses!

Q   What is big, red and eats rocks?
A   A big, red, rock eater!

Q   Why is a cook bad?
A   Because she beats eggs!

Knock, knock.
Q   Who's there?
A   Isabel.
Q   Isabel who?
A   Is a bel(l) necessary on a bicycle?

Q   Why is it useless to send letters to Washington?
A   Because he is dead!

Q   What is the difference between a hill and a pill?
A   One is hard to get up and the other is hard to get down!

Q   What is the hardest part of milking a mouse?
A   Getting a bucket under it!

Q   Which house should be easy to lift?
A   A lighthouse!

Q   What were Batman and Robin known as when they were run over by a steam roller?
A   Flatman and Ribbon!

Q   What is the best butter in the world?
A   A goat!

Q   How do porcupines kiss?
A   Very carefully!

Q   What did one candle say to the other candle?
A   'Let's go out tonight!'

Q   What is an Eskimo's
    tooth called?
A   A polar molar!

Q   What should you call an
    accountant smoking a pipe?
A   A puff adder!

Q   Why do giraffes have that
    no other animal has?
A   Baby giraffes!

Q   What is yellow and writes under water?
A   A ball-point banana!

Q   How does a dinosaur tell another dinosaur to hurry
    up!
A   Pronto Saurus!

Q   When is a restaurant like a wood shed?
A   When it's a chop house!

Q   What is yellow, soft and goes round and round?
A   A long-playing omelette!

Q   What is the worst weather for rats and mice?
A   When it's raining cats and dogs!

Q   What do you give a sick bird?
A   The tweetment!

    Knock knock.
Q   Who's there?
A   Dwayne.
Q   Dwayne who?
A   Dwayne the swimming pool, I'm sinking!

Q When is a door not a door?
A When it's a jar (ajar)!

Q What goes up and down but stays in one place?
A A road!

Q What is most useful when it is broken?
A An egg!

Q What do you hold but do not touch?
A Your breath!

Q When is a piece of wood like a queen?
A When it's a ruler!

Q Which was the first bus to cross the Atlantic?
A Columbus!

Q Why is twice eleven the same as twice ten?
A Twice eleven is twenty-two and twice ten is twenty, too!

Q What is worse than a giraffe with a sore neck?
A A centipede with sore feet!

Q What is the best way to catch a squirrel?
A Climb a tree and act like a nut!

Q What is big, red and eats sand?
A A big, red rock eater on a diet!

Q What did the young rose say to the other young rose?
A 'Hiya, bud!'

Q What did one wall say to the other wall?
A 'I'll meet you at the corner!'

Q Why was six sad at dinner?
A Because seven ate (eight) nine!

Q What goes up a down pipe down but won't go up an up pipe up?
A An umbrella!

Q What time is it if an elephant sits on a fence?
A Time to get a new fence!

Q If you had two parrots, one red and one green, which flew into a tree and a very silly person got the red one down but not the green one, what would he say when you asked him why he only got the red one down?
A 'The green one isn't ripe yet!'

Q What did the mayonnaise say to the lettuce?
A 'Shut the door, I'm dressing!'

Q What is clean when it is black and white when it is dirty?
A A blackboard!

Q   Why do elephants have ivory tusks?
A   Because wooden ones would rot!

Q   Why do bees buzz?
A   Because they can't sing!

Q   If you lost your arm in an accident where would you go?
A   To a second hand shop!

Q   Where should you put a monster on a goods train?
A   In the freight (fright) car!

Q   What is another name for a ghost ship?
A   Witch craft!

Q   What is nothing?
A   A balloon with the skin scraped off!

Q   Why couldn't the viper viper nose?
A   The adder adder handkerchief!

Q   Which is the left side of a chocolate cake?
A   The side you haven't eaten yet!

Q   What do you grow in a garden if you work hard?
A   Tired!

Q   Why do you look over a stone wall?
A   Because you can't look through it!

Q   What plant can give you a scare?
A   A creeper!

Q   What would you have if you crossed a hedgehog with a giraffe?
A   A long-handled brush!

Q   What is hard to beat?
A   A drum with a hole in it!

Q   Why didn't the army go to war?
A   Because there was a general strike!

Q   What is the most romantic fruit salad?
A   A date with a peach!

Q   How would you divide fourteen apples among fifteen people?
A   Make apple sauce!

Q   What did Michael Faraday say when he discovered electricity?
A   'How shocking!'

Q   If Mrs Ippi lent Miss Ouri her New Jersey what will Dela wear?
A   I'll ask her (Alaska)!

Q   What is the difference between a hunted deer and a witch?
A   One is a hunted stag and the other is a stunted hag!

Q What thing of yours do other people use more than you do yourself?
A Your name!

Q How can you learn to read in the dark?
A By going to night school!

Q What did mother bee say to baby bee?
A Behave (beehive) yourself!

Q What is the biggest verse there is?
A The universe!

Q How did the octopus go into battle?
A Well-armed!

Q Why was the bull dozer square?
A Because it couldn't dig that crazy rock!

Q How would a cake of soap help if your boat sank?
A You could use it to wash yourself ashore!

Q What are the best book markers?
A Jammy fingers!

Q Why did the chicken cross the road?
A To get away from Colonel Sanders!

Q Why did the chicken *not* cross the road?
A It was foul (fowl) on the other side!

Q If there was a candle on the table, a candle in the window, a woodburning stove and you only had one match which would you light first?
A The match!

Q   Who may marry many a wife but still stay single?
A   A minister!

Q   During the day we breathe oxygen, what should we breathe at night?
A   Nitrogen (night-rogen)!

Knock knock.
Q   Who's there?
A   Sam and Janet.
Q   Sam and Janet who?
A   Sam and Janet Evening (Some enchanted evening)!

Q   There were ten men in a boat. The boat tipped over and nine men got their hair wet. Why didn't the tenth get his hair wet?
A   He was bald!

Q   What did Tarzan say when he saw a herd of elephants wearing sun glasses?
A   Nothing. He didn't recognise them!

Q   Why did the elephant leave its job at the circus?
A   It got tired of working for peanuts!

Q   How do you know when there is an elephant in your bed?
A   It has an 'E' on its pyjamas!

Q Why can't an elephant ride a bike?
A Because it has no fingers to ring the bell!

Q Why did Mickey Mouse run away from home?
A Because his father was a rat!

Q What does Batman wear when he goes for a bath?
A A bath-robe (bat-robe)!

Q What is the monster's favourite ballet?
A Swan Lake (Swamp Lake)!

Q What were the baby monster's parents called?
A Dad and Mummy (Dead and Mummy)!

Q What is the pop idol's hobby?
A Collecting fans!

Q What starts with a P and ends with an E and has hundreds of letters in it?
A A post office!

Q Why are pretty girls like door hinges?
A Because they are things to a door (adore)!

Q What may a cat have six of and a dog has none?
A Kittens!

Q What is black and white and red all over?
A An embarrassed zebra!

Q What did the spaceman see in the frying pan?
A An unidentified frying object!

Q Why are a boy and a crab the same?
A They both go red when they get into hot water!

Q A lady fell down a well. How did she get out?
A She had a ladder in her stocking!

Q Why is a dog's tail like the heart of a tree?
A Because it is farthest from the bark!

Q Which bird nests in your throat?
A The swallow!

Q Why can hens only lay eggs in the day time?
A Because at night they are roosters!

Q Which shoe do you always take off last!
A The one which is left!

Q What fruit do you find on a penny?
A The date!

Q What did the curtain say to the window?
A 'I can see through you!'

Q On which day of the week is ice cream most likely to melt?
A Sunday (sun-day)!

Q What keeps hot all the year round?
A Mustard!

Q What is the best day for cooking?
A Friday (fry day)!

Q Why is a snake a careless animal?
A Because it keeps losing its skin!

Q What table is made of paper?
A A time table!

Q Which American state is tall in the middle and round at both ends?
A Ohio (O high O)!

Q Two people were crossing a bridge. One was the father of the other's son. What relation were they to each other?
A Husband and wife!

Q What can a person always count on?
A His fingers!

Q When did the Irish potato change its nationality?
A When it became a French fry!

Q Why is a rooster always neat?
A Because he carries a comb with him!

Q What is a wise-cracker?
A A smart cookie!

Q Why didn't the worms go into Noah's Ark in pairs?
A Because they wanted to go in apples!

Q What are unmarried hippopotamuses called?
A Hippopotamisses!

Q Why are the hours one to twelve like a good policeman?
A Because they are always on the watch!

Q   How many balls of string would it take to reach the moon?
A   One. But it would have to be long enough!

Q   What is worse than a howling cat stuck in a tree?
A   Two howling cats stuck in a tree!

Q   If your white hat got blown in the Red Sea, what would you get?
A   A wet hat!

Q   Why did the man put his transistor in the refrigerator?
A   He wanted to hear cool music!

Q   What animal would you like to see on a cold day?
A   A little otter (hotter)!

Q   What would you call a little Indian joke?
A   A mini ha ha!

Q   What is always before you but cannot be seen?
A   The future.

Q   What passes through a door but never leaves the room?
A   A key hole!

Q   What did one Christmas cracker say to the other Christmas cracker?
A   'My pop is bigger than your pop!'

Q   What did one fountain say to the other fountain?
A   'Hiya, squirt!'

Q When is a black dog not a black dog?
A When it's a greyhound!

Q Why does a horse have six legs?
A Because it has two legs at
the back and four (fore)
legs in front!

Q What can't you have for
dinner or tea?
A Breakfast!

Q Where was the Magna Carta signed?
A At the bottom!

Q What can a person hold in his right hand but not in
his left?
A His left elbow!

Q Why is a banana like a sweater?
A Because you slip on both!

Q What is the difference between a donkey and a
stamp?
A One you lick with a stick and the other you stick
with a lick!

Q Why do birds fly south in winter?
A It is too far to walk!

Q Why do bees buzz?
A Because they can't whistle!

Q Why did the elephant paint its toenails red and its
body green?
A So it could hide in a cherry tree!

Q How did the ten-year-old boy get a driving licence?
A He drove his mother up the wall!

Q Why did the old lady put wheels on her rocking chair?
A She wanted to rock and roll!

Q What would you do if you wore your trousers out?
A You would wear them back home again!

Q What do monsters do at 10.30?
A They take a coffee (coffin) break!

Q What would you call a neat, handsome, kind-hearted monster?
A A failure!

Q Why did the thief take a bath?
A Because he couldn't make a clean getaway!

Q What travels under water at 60 m.p.h.?
A A motorpike!

Q What word of ten letters can be spelled with five?
A Expediency (XPDNC)!

Q Which King of France wore the biggest shoes?
A The king with the biggest feet!

Q What would you get if you crossed a bumble bee with a door bell?
A A humdinger!

Q A girl in a sweet shop was one metre fifty centimetres tall and wore size five shoes. What did she weigh?
A Sweets!

Q What is green and hairy and goes up and down?
A A gooseberry in a lift!

Q What is black, wrinkled and glows?
A An electric prune!

Q What is white outside, green inside and hops?
A A frog sandwich!

Q What did the active volcano shout when his girl friend left him?
A 'Lava (lover) come back!'

Q Why was the cross-eyed teacher sacked?
A She couldn't control her pupils!

Q One man made it but didn't use it. One man bought it but didn't use it. One man needed it but could neither see nor feel it. What was it?
A A coffin!

Q Why did the boy cross the road, wash his hands, cross the road, wash his hands?
A Because he was a dirty, double crosser!

Q What is as big as an elephant but weighs nothing?
A An elephant's shadow!

Q When is soup like a gold ring?
A When it has eighteen carrots (carats)!

Q What did the elephant say to the banana?
A 'Let's play squash!'

Q What horse can't you ride?
A A clothes horse!

Q What bean does not grow in soil?
A A jelly bean!

Q Why is a butcher who takes down a leg of pork from a shelf to be pitied?
A Because he's a poor creature (pork reacher)!

Q What is a zookey?
A The key to a zoo!

Q What has four eyes yet cannot see?
A The Mississippi!

Q What is purple and swims in the ocean?
A Mauvy Dick!

Q What band never plays music?
A A hat band!

Q Who is a square cowboy?
A Hop-a-long (Oblong) Cassidy!

Q What has one horn and gives milk?
A A milk truck!

Q Why did the jam roll?
A Because it saw the apple turnover!

Q Why did the jelly wobble?
A Because it saw the milk shake!

Q What do you call a lady boss?
A Miss Chief (Mischief)!

Q Why should you never be hungry in the desert?
A Because of the sand which (sandwich) is there!

Q Which is the strongest day of the week?
A Sunday. All the rest are week (weak) days!

Q What are the largest ants?
A Giants!

Q Which is the longest word in the English language?
A Smiles, because there is a mile between the two Ss!

Q Why was Cinderella dropped from the cricket team?
A Because she ran away from the ball!

Q Three tomatoes were on a fence. Which one was the
   cowboy?
A None, they were all redskins!

Q What swims in the water and paints?
A Leonardo da Fishy!

Q What goes, zzub, zzub?
A A bee flying backwards!

Q What has one eye, one leg, picks
   cotton and plucks chickens?
A A one-eyed, one legged, cotton picking chicken
   plucker!

Q   Why is a lame dog like a schoolboy adding six and seven?
A   Because he puts down three and carries one!

Q   Where would you find an elephant?
A   It depends on where you lost him!

Q   What weighs a ton and is covered in hair?
A   A hippopotamus (hippy-potamus)!

Q   What do you call a line of people waiting at a hairdresser's?
A   A barber queue (barbecue)!

Q   What do bees do with their honey?
A   They sell (cell) it!

Q   What did the gas fire say to the coin?
A   'Thanks for dropping in, I was just thinking of going out!'

Q   Why did the coal scuttle?
A   Because it saw the kitchen sink!

Q   What plant do two hedgehogs represent?
A   A prickly pear (pair)!

Q   Why is the bride unhappy on her wedding day?
A   Because she does not marry the best man!

Q   What did the clown say to the three-headed monster?
A   'Hello, hello, hello!'

Q   Why is good bread like the sun?
A   Because it is light when it rises!

Q   What did the Soviet satellite say to the moon?
A   'Don't stop me, I'm rushin'!' (Russian)

Q   Why aren't there any telephones in China?
A   Because there are too many Wings and too many
    Wongs and it would mean that somebody would
    wing the wong number!

Q   Why did the fly, fly?
A   Because the spider spied her!

Q   Which word of five letters is longer than a word of
    ten letters?
A   'Metre' is longer than 'centimetre'!

Q   Why did the elephant
    cross the road?
A   Because it was the
    chicken's day off!

Q   Why did Tommy bring
    his mini-bike to school?
A   To drive teacher up the wall!

Q   Why does a successful thief never worry?
A   Because he takes things easy!

Q   What is the difference between a teacher and a train?
A   The teacher says, 'Throw that gum away.' The train
    says, 'Choo, Choo' (chew, chew)!

Q   Why is a match brave?
A   Because it never complains when it is struck!

Q   What did Mr Flea say to Mrs Flea?
A   'Shall we take a walk, or a dog?'

Q   What is a meat ball?
A   A dance at a butcher's shop!

Q   What did the Abominable Snowman say when he
    saw the rooster lay an egg?
A   'Himalaya!' (Him, a layer!)

Q   Why do people laugh up their sleeve?
A   Because that is where their funny bone is!

Q   Take off my skin and I won't cry, but you will. What
    am I?
A   I'm an onion!

Q   When is it dangerous to go in the garden?
A   When the young plants are shooting!

Q   Which animal wins its fights unfairly?
A   The cheetah (cheater)!

Q   What kind of salt is not used at table?
A   Somersault!

Q   Put three ducks in a crate
    and what do you have?
A   A box of quackers!

Q   When is a fish like a bird?
A   When it takes a fly!

Q   What is the favourite
    fruit of history?
A   Dates!

Q   Why can a one-eyed man see more than a two-eyed man?
A   The two-eyed man can only see a man with one eye, but the one-eyed man can see a man with two eyes!

Q   What is the difference between a wet day and a boy being spanked?
A   The wet day pours with rain and the boy roars with pain!

Q   What did the robot say to the petrol pump?
A   'Take your finger out of your ear and listen to me!'

Q   Why is a giraffe a small eater?
A   Because he makes a little go a long way!

Q   How do you make a band stand?
A   Take their chairs away!

Q   What do crocodiles do when they are bored?
A   Play snap!

Knock, knock.
Q   Who's there?
A   Mary.
Q   Mary who?
A   Mary Christmas (Merry Christmas)!

Q   What goes up and never comes down?
A   Your age!

Q   What disappears when you stand up?
A   Your lap!

Q   What goes, kiss, ouch, kiss ouch! ?
A   Two porcupines kissing!

Q When is a motor car
like a baby?
A When it has a rattle!

Q Why are fish so smart?
A Because they always
go round in schools!

Q What is yellow and white and travels at 60 m.p.h.?
A An egg sandwich on the Scottish Express!

Q What has four legs and flies?
A Two birds!

Q Why did the little girl leave the party?
A Because she was fed up!

Q Why did the boy throw his watch out of the window?
A Because he wanted to see time fly!

Q Why is it hard to tell someone a secret if you have a
pet goat?
A Because the goat keeps butting in!

Q Why did the orange stop in the middle of the road?
A Because it ran out of juice!

Q What is the difference between a hare and a rabbit?
A A rabbit can grow hairs (hares) but a hare can't grow
rabbits!

Q What is a cannibal?
A A person who goes to a restaurant and orders the
waiter!

Q Why did Napoleon wear his hat sideways?
A Military strategy. He didn't want the enemy to know which way he was going!

Q Why did the small boy think the bank was a television studio?
A Because he heard his father say that was where the Lone Ranger (loan arranger) was!

Q Which sea is like a well-built upper storey?
A Adriatic (a dry attic)!

Q Would you rather go hungry or have seven holes in your head?
A You already have seven holes in your head!

Q What has seven legs, no head and a tail?
A A cat eating out of an iron pot!

Q What has ears like a cat, a head like a cat, feet like a cat, a tail like a cat, but isn't a cat?
A A kitten!

Q What is taller sitting than standing?
A A dog!

Q What is blacker than a crow?
A Its feathers!

Q What wears a coat all winter and pants in the summer?
A A dog!

Q Why can't a bike stand up by itself?
A Because it is too tired (two-tyred)!

Q To whom does every man raise his hat?
A His barber!

Q Which kind of boat
resembles a knife?
A A cutter!

Q What is there at the
end of everything?
A The letter 'g'!

Q Which is easier to spell, fiddle-de-dee, or fiddle-de-dum?
A Fiddle-de-dee, because it is spelled with more ease (E's)!

Q Which of the heavenly bodies cannot find suitable lodgings?
A The moon, because it is always changing quarters!

Q Which is the most dangerous kind of bat that flies through the air?
A The brick bat!

Q Which Member of Parliament wears the largest hat?
A The one with the largest head!

Q Which South American country are you reminded of when there's a coal strike?
A Chile (chilly)!

When and what?

Q When is a nose not a nose?
A When it is dripping!

Q When does a dog like the rain?
A When it begins to patter (pat her) on the back!

Q When does a Scotsman behave like an ass?
A When he walks to the banks and braes (brays)!

Q When is a boy not a boy?
A When he is a little pale (pail)!

Q When do elephants have eight feet?
A When there are two of them!

Q When is a road like the letter 't'?
A When it is crossed!

Q What time is it when the engine-driver blows his whistle?
A It is two-to-two (toot-toot-to)!

Q When you get out of bed in the morning which continent are you in?
A Europe (you're up)!

Q When does a leopard change its spots?
A When it goes to live in another place!

Q Which animal needs oiling?
A A mouse when it squeaks!

Q   When is a doctor angry?
A   When he loses his patience
    (patients)!

Q   When is a public speaker
    like a pony?
A   When he becomes a little
    hoarse (horse)!

Q   What is the best material with which to cover a
    chair?
A   It has to be satin (sat in)!

Q   When was meat the highest it has ever been?
A   When the cow jumped over the moon!

Q   Why is it dangerous to keep a clock upstairs?
A   It might run down and strike one!

Q   When can your pocket be empty and still have
    something in it?
A   When it has a hole in it!

Q   When are your eyes not eyes?
A   When the wind makes them water!

Q   When does a farmer make magic?
A   When he turns his horse to grass and his cows to
    pasture!

Q   What is the best way for a father to let his children
    know he has just come home from work?
A   Walk in front of the television set!

Q   What did the man reply when he was asked who he
    worked for?
A   'A wife and six kids!'

Q   What colour should you paint the sun and the wind?
A   The sun rose and the wind blew (blue)!

Q   What is the best way to raise turnips?
A   Take hold of the leaves and pull!

Q   What did the midget say when the dwarf asked to borrow a pound?
A   'I can't, I'm short myself!'

Q   What would you do if you had only one pound in the world?
A   Buy a wallet to put it in!

Q   What did one ear say to the other ear?
A   'Meet you round the block!'

Q   What do you give away and still keep?
A   A bad cold!

Q   What is a friend?
A   A person who has the same enemies as yourself!

Q   At what time when you have something to give, will no one come near you?
A   When you have whooping cough!

Q   When is a boat like a heap of snow?
A   When it is adrift (a drift)!

Q   When is a lady not a lady?
A   When she turns into a store!

Q   What opens the gates to the cemetery?
A   A skeleton key!

Q   What are the three quickest ways of spreading the
    news?
A   Telephone, telegram and tell a girl!

Q   What is found in the very centre of Australia and
    and America?
A   The letter 'r'?

Q   What did Tennessee?
A   I don't know but it was the same as Arkansas
    (Arkan-saw)!

Q   What has four legs, a head but only one foot?
A   A bed!

Q   What would happen to you if you swallowed a
    teaspoon?
A   You wouldn't be able to stir!

Q   What is the easiest thing
    for a miser to part with?
A   A comb!

Q   What do you take off last
    when you go to bed?
A   The last things you take off are your feet from off
    the floor!

Q   What liquid is necessary for both a motor car and a
    freighter?
A   Petrol, because it makes the cargo (car go)!

Q   What is there about a skating rink that reminds you
    of a Court of Law?
A   Justice (Just ice)!

Q What is the best thing to put in a Christmas pudding?
A Your teeth!

Q What do you break when you say its name?
A Silence!

Q What did Dick Turpin say to his horse Black Bess when he arrived in York after his famous ride?
A 'Whoa!'

Q What has eyes but cannot see?
A A potato!

Q What is always behind time?
A The back of a watch!

Q What has a tongue but makes no sound?
A A shoe!

Q What has legs but cannot walk?
A A table, or chair!

Q What should you keep even after you have given it to someone else?
A A promise!

Q What goes from Lands End to John o' Groats but never moves?
A A road!

Q What is everyone in the world doing at the same time?
A Growing older!

Q What is always coming but never arrives?
A Tomorrow.

Q What do you need most in the long run?
A Your breath!

Q What does everyone want but likes to get rid of as soon as possible?
A A good appetite!

Q What works when it plays and plays when it works?
A A fountain!

Q What always walks with its head down?
A A nail in your shoe!

Q What gets longer the more you cut off it?
A A ditch!

Q What is it we all say we will do, tell others to do, but have never done it?
A Stop a minute!

Q What stays hot even in the fridge?
A Mustard!

Q What is a Laplander?
A A clumsy man on a bus!

Q What man can raise things without lifting them?
A A gardener!

Q What kind of clothes last the longest?
A Underwear because they are never worn out!

Q What is smaller than the mouth of an ant?
A The food the ant eats!

Riddles in the garden

Q What vegetable should be valued with diamonds?
A Carrots (carats)!

Q What fruit might give you a shock?
A A currant (current)!

Q What fruit is found in twos?
A Pears (pairs)!

Q What vegetable would
you find in a crowded bus?
A A squash!

Q What vegetable do you like to get from your pen pal?
A Lettuce (letters)!

Q What vegetable might grow on your toe?
A Corn!

Q What vegetable needs a new washer?
A A leek (leak)!

Q What vegetable makes the most money?
A The mint!

Q What fruit would you find in a newspaper?
A The date!

Q   What flower does everyone grow?
A   Tulips (two lips)!

Q   What flower do you find where there are a lot of birds?
A   Phlox (flocks)!

Q   What flower is like an icy wind?
A   Freesia (Freeze ya)!

Q   What three flowers sound like a proposal of marriage?
A   Sweet William, rose and aster (Sweet William, rose and asked her)!

Q   Before a girl marries a man which flower does she ask for?
A   Anemone (any money?)!

A swarm of ants

Questions
1   What is a page boy ant?
2   What is a plentiful ant?
3   What is a needy ant?
4   What is a graceful ant?
5   What is an enormous ant?
6   What is a wandering ant?
7   What is a stupid ant?
8   What is a sweet-smelling ant?
9   What is a sloping ant?
10 What is a gasping ant?

Answers
1   Attendant
2   Abundant
3   Want
4   Elegant
5   Elephant or Giant
6   Vagrant
7   Ignorant
8   Fragrant
9   Slant
10 Pant

Words, words, words

Q What word of six letters contains six other words besides itself, without altering the position of any of the letters?

A Herein: He, her, here, ere, rein, in!

Q There is a word of three syllables from which if you take away five letters a male remains. If you take away four letters a female remains. If you take away three letters you are left with a brave man and the whole word means a brave woman. What is it?

A Heroine: (He, her, hero)!

Q In a certain word L is near the middle, is at the beginning and at the end. But there is only one L in the whole word. What is it?

A Island. 'L' is near the middle, 'is' is at the beginning and 'and' is at the end!

Q Is there a word in the English language that contains all the vowels?

A Unquestionably!

Q What word is it from which the whole can be taken and some will remain?
A Wholesome!

Q What two words in the English language contain all the vowels in their proper order. That is, a e i o u ?
A Facetious and abstemious!

Q Can you write a composition using two letters only?
A S.A. (essay)

Q A Red Indian wigwam can be spelt with two letters. What are they?
A T.P. (tepee)

Q There are eleven letters in 'deteriorate'. Can you explain what it means with only two letters?
A D.K. (decay)

Q Spell the name of a climbing plant that clings to the wall. Use only two letters.
A I.V. (ivy)

Q What two letters mean jealousy?
A N.V. (envy)

Q Which English county can you spell with two letters?
A S.X. (Essex)

Q Spell 'pretty girl' with only two letters.
A Q.T. (cutie)

Riddles in the alphabet

Q Why is the letter E unhappy?
A Because it is always in misery and never in good spirits!

Q Why is the letter A like pollen?
A Because a B comes after it!

Q Why is the letter D like a lazy husband?
A Because it makes ma mad!

Q Why is O the noisiest vowel?
A Because A, E, I and U are inaudible (in audible)!

Q What starts with T and ends with T and is full of T?
A A tea-pot!

Q How does the letter A help a deaf woman?
A It makes her hear!

Q What word of three syllables contains twenty-six letters?
A Alphabet!

Q What letter separates Ireland from England?
A C (sea)!

Q Which are the cleverest letters?
A The Ys (the wise)!

Q Can you list ten ways of spelling the sound of the the letter O?

A (1) O as in go. (2) Owe as in owe. (3) Oe as in toe. (4) Oa as in boat. (5) Eau as in beau. (6) Oh as in Oh! (7) Ough as in dough. (8) Ow as in snow. (9) Ot as in jabot. (10) Ew as in sew!

Q Why is the letter A like lunch?

A Because both are in the middle of the day!

Q Why is the letter E unlucky?

A Because it is always in debt, always out of cash and always in danger!

Q Tommy Tucker took two strings to tie together two tired turtles, two tall tropical trees and ten tiny toes. How many T's are there in that?

A There are only two T's in 'that'!

Q Constantinople is a very hard word, can you spell it?

A I-t spells 'it'!

Q What letter is never found in the alphabet?

A The one you put in the mail!

Q How do you spell 'hungry horse' in four letters?

A M T G G (empty gee gee)!

Q   Why is U the happiest letter?
A   Because it is always in the middle of fun!

Q   Why should men avoid the letter A?
A   Because it makes men mean!

Q   Why is the letter P like a Roman Emperor?
A   Because it is near O (Nero)!

Q   Why is the letter E like London?
A   Because it is the capital of England!

Q   Why is the letter D like a sailor?
A   Because it follows the C (sea)!

Q   Which three large bodies of water would you find in
     a coloured poster?
A   The Red Sea, the Black Sea and the White Sea
     (red C, black C and the white C)!

Q   Which letter will spell 'potatoes'?
A   The letter O. Write it down one at a time till you
     have 'put eight O's' (potatoes)!

Riddles a little bird told me

Q Which is the saddest bird?
A The blue bird!

Q Which bird lifts heavy weights?
A The crane!

Q Which bird gets run over by a train?
A The rail!

Q Which is the rudest bird?
A The mocking bird!

Q Which bird do you find in the aphabet?
A The jay!

Q Which bird flies around at meal times?
A The swallow!

Q Which bird would you find in a cathedral?
A The cardinal!

Q Which bird sits on a chess board?
A The rook!

Q Which bird keeps facing about?
A The tern (turn)!

Q Which is a foolish bird?
A The cuckoo!

Q   Which bird holds up a flower?
A   The stork (stalk)!

Q   Which bird thinks it is a rooster?
A   The crow!

Q   Which bird tells untruths?
A   The lyre bird (liar bird)!

Q   Which bird plays pranks?
A   The lark!

Q   Which bird likes to go out in the dark in a storm?
A   The nightingale (night in gale)!

Q   Which bird will dodge if you aim a blow at it?
A   The duck!

Q   Which bird moves very quickly?
A   The swift!

Q   Which bird makes a noise like a tom cat?
A   The emu (he mew)!

Q   Which bird works under water?
A   The diver!

Q   Which bird is a royal angler?
A   The kingfisher!

Riddles from the Bible

Q Who was the most successful doctor in the Bible?
A Job, because he had the most patients (patience)!

Q Who was the most successful actor in the Bible?
A Samson, because he brought down the house!

Q What was the time when Adam was created?
A A little before Eve!

Q When was radio mentioned in the Bible?
A When God took a rib from Adam and made a loud speaker (Eve)!

Q Why couldn't Eve have measles?
A Because she'd had 'em (Adam)!

Q Which animals took luggage with them when they went into the Ark?
A The elephant took a trunk, the fox took a brush and the cock took a comb!

Q Why was Samson unlucky?
A He died of fallen arches!

Q Why were Adam and Eve noisy people and lucky to have no neighbours?
A Because they raised Cain!

Q Did Eve ever have a date with Adam?
A No, it was an apple!

Q How long did Cain hate his brother?
A Just as long as he was able (Abel)!

Q When is tennis mentioned in the Bible?
A When it says that Joseph served in Pharaoh's court!

Q When are pills mentioned in the Bible?
A When the Lord gave Moses two tablets!

Q Why did Adam bite the apple?
A Because he didn't have a knife!

Q How do you know Noah was not the first out of the Ark when it came to rest on the mountain?
A Because it says Noah came forth (fourth)!

Q When Adam first met Eve, he was so excited at seeing a girl for the first time that he didn't know whether he was coming or going. So he introduced himself with a sentence that reads the same backwards as forwards. What was it?
A 'Madam, I'm Adam!'

Q Why had Noah to be careful when he fished from the Ark?
A Because he only had two worms!

Q Where was Noah when the light went out?
A In the dark (d-ark)!

Q Why do we think that Moses wore a wig?
A Because he was sometimes seen with hair on (Aaron) and sometimes without!

Q Which man in the Bible had no parents?
A It was Joshua, the son of Nun (none)!

Q What did the stuttering cat say when the Ark came to rest on the mountain?

A 'Is that A ra-rat?' (Ararat)!

Q Who was the best runner in the Bible?

A Adam. He was the first in the human race!

Q Why was Goliath surprised when David hit him with a stone?

A Because such a thing had never before entered his head!

Q Who was the strongest man in the Bible? Stronger even than Samson?

A Jonah, because the whale couldn't hold him even after it had got him down!

Q Which are the two smallest things mentioned in the Bible?

A The widow's mite and the wicked flea (flee)!

Q What was the longest day in the Bible?

A The one when there was no Eve in it!

A bouquet of flowers

Questions
1. What flower is a common household implement?
2. What flower is a bird that swears?
3. What flower is a well-dressed wild animal?
4. What flower is a white globule of moisture?
5. What flower is a coloured ringer?
6. What flower is worn in winter?
7. What flower is a vehicle and country?
8. What flower is a stumbling animal?
9. What flower is an animal and something to wear?
10. What flower is a game and a fabulous animal?

Answers
1. Broom
2. Crocus (crow cuss)
3. Dandelion (dandy lion)
4. Snowdrop
5. Bluebell
6. Furze (furs)
7. Carnation
8. Cowslip
9. Foxglove
10. Snapdragon

A number of riddles

Q   Why is the figure 9 like a peacock?
A   Because without its tail it would be nothing (0)!

Q   Why should the number 288 never be mentioned in polite society?
A   It is too gross (two gross)!

Q   What is the difference between 100 and 1000?
A   Nothing (0)!

Q   What two numbers multiplied together will give you seven?
A   Seven and one!

Q   How many times can seven be subtracted from 650?
A   Only once because after the first subtraction the number ceases to be 650!

Q   From what number can you take half and leave nothing?
A   8. If you take away the top half, o is left behind!

Q   What is the difference between twice twenty-two and twice two and twenty?
A   Twice twenty-two is forty-four and twice two and twenty is four plus twenty which is twenty-four!

Q   If you add eight eights together the answer is 64. Can you add eight eights together so that the answer is 1000?
A $888+88+8+8+8$!

Some riddles from history

Q Why are the Middle Ages called the Dark Ages?
A Because there are so many nights (knights) in them!

Q How was Henry VIII different from other husbands?
A He married his wives before he asked (axed) them!

Q Which letter of the Alphabet is most like Julius, the Emperor of Rome?
A The Cs are (Caesar)!

Q Why did William Tell's son feel relieved after his father shot the apple off his head?
A Because he had a narrow escape (an arrow escape)!

Q Why is the history of England like a wet summer?
A Because it is full of reigns (rains)!

Q Why could King John never draw a straight line?
A Because he was a bad ruler!

Q Which bird was the first to go round the world?
A A Drake!

Q What did the ruler of Russia say when he was crowned?
A 'I've an (Ivan) Empire!'

A flock of birds

Questions
1 What bird appears when you have finished chewing?
2 What bird would dodge if you threw a stone at it?
3 What bird likes to boast?
4 What bird is the ruler of the anglers?
5 What bird would sell things in the street?
6 What bird flies high over the moor?
7 What bird gets up to mischief?
8 What bird is an abbreviated periodical and something good to eat?
9 What bird is a vegetable and a male?
10 What bird would be equally bad with another?

Answers
1 Swallow
2 Duck
3 Crow
4 Kingfisher
5 Hawk
6 Starling
7 Lark
8 Magpie
9 Peacock
10 Parrot (par rot)

What is the difference?

Q What is the difference between a church bell and a thief?

A The bell peals from the steeple and the thief steals from the people!

Q What is the difference between the King's eldest son, a bald man and a monkey's mother?

A The King's son is the heir apparent. The bald man has no hair apparent. And the monkey's mother is a hairy parent!

Q What is the difference between a black cloud and a wounded lion?

A The black cloud pours with rain and the wounded lion roars with pain!

Q What is the difference between a cat and a comma?

A The cat has claws at the end of its paws and the comma makes a pause at the end of a clause!

Q What is the difference between a crazy hare and a counterfeit note?

A The crazy hare is a mad bunny and the counterfeit note is bad money!

Q   What is the difference between a bus driver and a cold in the head?
A   One knows the stops and the other stops the nose!

Q   What is the difference between a postage stamp and a girl?
A   The postage stamp is a mail fee and the girl is a female!

Q   What is the difference between the church bell and the organ?
A   The bell will ring when it is told (tolled) but the organ will be blowed first!

Q   What is the difference between a twelve year old boy and his father taking a nap?
A   The boy is twelve and his father is a-dozin' (a dozen)!

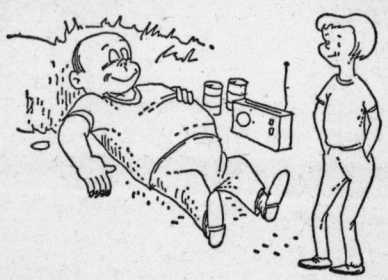

Q   What is the difference between a teacher and a railway guard?
A   The teacher trains the mind and the guard minds the train!

Q   What is the difference between a piano, a ship on a
    choppy sea and you?
A   The piano makes music, the ship on the choppy sea
    makes you sick and you make me sick (only try this
    one on your friends)!

Q   What is the difference between a very rich man, an
    orang-utan and a glue pot?
A   The very rich man is a millionaire and the orang-
    utan has a million hairs!
Q   But what about the glue pot?
A   That's where we get stuck!

Q   What is the difference between a baby and a ship-
    wrecked sailor?
A   The baby clings to its ma, and the sailor clings to his
    spar (pa)!

Why, oh why?

Q Why is a bad boy like a dirty rug?
A Because they both need a beating!

Q Why is your pocket money like a secret?
A Because it is hard to keep!

Q Why is a ride in an aeroplane like falling down stairs?
A Because it makes you soar (sore)!

Q Why is an empty room like a room with a married couple in it?
A Because it doesn't contain a single person!

Q Why is a piece of bread, two weeks old like a rabbit running down its hole?
A Because you can see it's stale (its tail)!

Q Why is a game of cricket like a pancake?
A Because it depends on the batter!

Q Why are pop concerts like jewellers?
A Because they can make an ear ring (earring)!

Q Why is Christmas cake like the sea?
A Because it is full of currants (currents)!

Q Why is an eider duck like a cow's tail?
A Because it grows down!

Q Why is a promise like an egg?
A Because it is easily broken!

Q Why does a bootblack resemble the sun?
A Because it's his job to shine!

Q Why is a bull in a china shop like a fire in the bush?
A Because the sooner it's put out the better!

Q Why do resolutions resemble girls who faint at a pop concert?
A Because the sooner they are carried out the better!

Q Why do laws resemble the ocean?
A Because it is the breakers that cause the trouble!

Q Why does a gardener resemble the writer of detective stories?
A Because he has to work at his plot!

Q Why is a badly sung song like an old man's head?
A Because it is often bawled (bald)!

Q   Why is a terrified girl like a kind lady at a party?
A   The terrified girl gives out high screams and the kind lady gives out ice creams!

Q   Why does a person with his eyes closed resemble a poor teacher?
A   Because he keeps his pupils in darkness!

Q   Why is a nice but inelegant girl like brown sugar?
A   Because she is sweet but unrefined!

Q   Why are most girls careless with their clothes?
A   Because if they get a new dress they wear it out the same day!

Q   Why are husbands like fires?
A   They go out when unattended!

Q   Why did the shy visitor always sing in the bath?
A   Because there was no lock on the door!

Q   Why is it easy to ask a favour of a horse with a sore throat?
A   Because it can't say neigh (nay)!

Q   Why is the hair on the top of your head grey before the hair in your beard?
A   Because it is about sixteen years older!

Q Why can't an Eskimo write with that finger? (Hold
   up one finger when you ask this riddle)
A Because he can only write with his own fingers!

Q Why is a pencil like a riddle?
A Because it is no good without a point!

Q Why can't a bride have a secret?
A Because there's always someone to give her away!

Q Why is life like the hardest riddle?
A Because you have to give it up in the end!

Q Why is a fire in a circus so destructive?
A Because it is intense (in tents)!

Q Why should a liar stay indoors?
A So no one will find him out!

Q Why does a chef wear a tall white hat?
A To cover his head!

Q Why does the statue of Nelson stand in Trafagar
   Square?
A Because it can't sit down!

Q Why does an elderly chef wear a tall white hat?
A To cover his tall white head!

Q Why doesn't Sweden send her cattle overseas?
A Because she keeps her stock home (Stockholm)!

Q Why is it difficult to travel in the Far East?
A Because there is only one coach in China (Cochin
   China)!

Q Why is a trip to Egypt only suitable for very old people?

A Because it is a senile (see Nile) thing to do!

Q Why would it be a bad thing for a lion to go to the beach on Christmas Eve?

A Because it would get sandy claws (Santa Claus)!

Q Why does a man who has just shaved look like a North American animal?

A Because he is bare (bear) faced!

Q Why can't it snow for two consecutive days?

A Because there is a night in between!

Q Why is your sense of touch upset when you are sick?

A Because you don't feel well!

Q Why did the carpenters find it hard to believe there was such a things as glass?

A Because they never saw it!

Q Why is an elderly gentleman like a motor car after a puncture?

A Because he is retired (re-tyred)!

Turning the tables

Questions
1 This is a table you can sell.
2 This table might send you to sleep.
3 This is a table you don't want.
4 This table you can't avoid.
5 This table is nice to taste.
6 This table you would find in the garden.
7 This table is very nice.
8 This table is very annoying.
9 This table is easy to remember.
10 This table is well-behaved.

Answers
1 Marketable
2 Comfortable
3 Unsuitable
4 Inevitable
5 Palatable
6 Vegetable
7 Delectable
8 Irritable
9 Unforgettable
10 Respectable

In Australia

Can you explain why

1   In Australia the ants are so big that many of them weigh a kilogramme. Some of them sit on logs and bark when kangaroos go by.

The reason: If weighed together, many of them would weigh a kilogramme, but you would need very many. Some ants do sit on logs, they also sit on the bark even when there are no kangaroos in sight.

2   An Australian doctor had a brother who went prospecting for gold in the Outback. But the prospector had no brother.

The reason: The Australian doctor was the prospector's sister.

3   In Australia there are cherry-coloured cats and rose-coloured dogs.

The reason: There are black cherries and white roses.

4   In Australia, ant hills are sometimes as tall as a house. Digger McIntosh, always goes to the tallest, takes off his shoes and jumps over them.

The reason: It's easy to jump over your shoes.

5   A bus ran off a bridge over the Murray river but no one was hurt.

The reason: The bus ran off the bridge at one end as usual and continued along the road.

6   Four men managed to get under one umbrella in Alice Springs and none of them got wet.

The reason: It wasn't raining.

7 At Dubbo, a farmer and his daughter, the
   policeman's wife and the policeman went for a walk
   round the farm. They found a hen's nest with four
   eggs in it. They each took an egg and left one in the
   nest.
The reason: There were only three people because the
   policeman's wife was also the farmer's daughter.

8 In Australia all the buses and trains stop on
   Tuesdays and Fridays.
The reason: To let the passengers get on and off.

9 In Australia on a clear night, you can see for at
   least 350,000 kilometres.
The reason: That is how far away the moon is.

Strange cities

Questions
1 Which city behaves strangely?
2 Which city is a savage city?
3 Which city is a wise city?
4 Which city is a shocking city?
5 Which city is a fast city?
6 Which city is a well-known city?
7 Which city is a quarrelsome city?
8 Which city is a bold city?
9 Which city is a stretched-out city?
10 Which city is a bad city?

Answers
1 Eccentricity
2 Ferocity
3 Sagacity
4 Electricity
5 Velocity
6 Publicity
7 Pugnacity
8 Audacity
9 Elasticity
10 Atrocity

Riddles my Grannie told me

Q   Over the water, under the water. Never touches the
    water. What is it?
A   An egg in a duck!

Q   Why is a postage stamp like a naughty boy?
A   It gets licked and stuck in a corner!

Q   Sir Lancelot had a pain. When and where was the
    pain?
A   In the middle of the
    night (knight)!

Q   What is black and white
    and red all over?
A   A newspaper (it is read
    all over)!

Q   Why is a goose like
    a motor horn?
A   Because they both
    go, 'Honk!'

Q   When is a sailor not a sailor?
A   When he's a-board!

Q   What is it that a man never wants but when he's got
    it he wouldn't part with it for a million pounds?
A   A bald head!

Q What did Nelson's ship, the *Victory*, weigh?
A Its anchor!

Q Which Irish county can you put in a bottle?
A Cork!

Q When should you take a cab?
A When it's hailing taxis!

Q To which question must you always answer 'yes'?
A 'What does Y-E-S spell?'

Q What question can never be answered truthfully by 'yes'?
A 'Are you asleep?'

Q What is most like a hen stealing?
A A cock robin (robbing)!

Q What will a calf be after it is one year old?
A Two years old!

Q What pets make the loudest noise?
A Trum-pets!

Q What is the hardest thing when learning to ride a bicycle?
A The road!

Q Which room can you not enter?
A The mushroom!

Q What driver never breaks the rules of the road?
A A screwdriver!

Q　Why does a steam locomotive never sit down?
A　Because it has a tender behind!

Q　Why are tall people more lazy than short people?
A　Because they are longer in bed!

Q　Why does lightning shock people?
A　Because it doesn't know how to conduct itself!

Q　Why is paper money more valuable than coins?
A　Because when you put it in your pocket you double
　　it and when you take it out you find it in creases
　　(increases)!

Q　Why does a bald-headed man need no keys?
A　Because he has no locks!

Q　Why would you be mad to swim in the river that
　　flows through Paris?
A　Because you would be insane (in Seine)!

Q　Why should you be careful about telling secrets
　　on a farm?
A　Because the corn has ears, the potatoes have eyes
　　and the beans talk (bean stalk)!

Q　Which is the best time for a lazy person to read
　　a book?
A　Between summer and winter because autumn turns
　　the leaves!

Q　Why should you tip-toe past the medicine chest?
A　So you won't wake the sleeping pills!

Q　Why is an empty purse always the same?
A　Because it knows no change!

Q Why should two men in a balloon be polite to each other?
A So they shouldn't fall out!

Q Why would a barber rather cut the hair of six men from Liverpool rather than one man from Glasgow?
A Because he would get six times as much money!

Q Why is an empty matchbox better than a full one?
A Because it is matchless!

Q Take away one letter, take away two letters, take away all my letters and I still remain what I was. What am I?
A A postman!

Q The more you take away, the bigger I become. What am I?
A A hole!

Q Why is a barefoot boy like an Eskimo?
A Because he has no shoes (snow shoes)!

Q If you spell 'to', t-o, and you spell 'too', t-o-o, and you spell 'two' t-w-o, how do you spell the second day of the week?
A M-O-N-D-A-Y. (Not, Tuesday!)

Q If a chick found an orange in the nest what do you think it might say?
A 'Oh, look at the orange mama laid (marmalade)!

Q   If you were fishing in the harbour and an enemy ship sailed in, what would you do?
A   You would pull up your line and sinker (sink her)!

Q   If you can raise a sack of potatoes in dry weather what would you raise in wet weather?
A   Your umbrella!

Q   If you had a quarrel with the man next door and he called you a little insect, would he be wrong?
A   Yes. An insect has six legs!

Q   If two's company and three's a crowd, what are four and five?
A   Nine!

Q   Why is a well-trained horse like a kind-hearted man?
A   He always stops at the sound of whoa (woe)!

Q   The dew was arguing with the sun. At last the sun could stand no more, what did he say?
A   'Oh, dry up!'

Q   What most resembles half a cheese?
A   The other half!

Q   What smells most in a chemist's shop?
A   Your nose!

Q   What makes the Tower of Pisa lean?
A   It never eats!

Q   Why was Queen Anne like a book?
A   She had several pages!

Q At what time do four hungry boys get a share of the pie?
A Quarter to one!

Q What kind of noise annoys an oyster?
A A noisy noise annoys an oyster!

Q Why are bellows like an insect?
A They make the fire fly (fire-fly)!

Q Where would you find the smallest bridge?
A At the top of your nose!

Q What does a hen do when it stands on one leg?
A Lifts up the other leg!

Q What was the strangest meal ever known?
A It started by a man bolting a door, then he swallowed a story whole and finally threw up a window!

Q Which figure in geometry resembles a lost bird?
A A polygon (a Polly gone)!

Q If you split your sides laughing, how could you get well again?
A Laugh some more till you were in stitches!

Q Which key is sometimes hard to turn?
A A don-key!

Q What makes more noise than a pig caught under a fence?
A Two pigs caught under a fence!

Q What is worse than finding a grub in an apple?
A Finding half a grub in an apple!

Q   Which roof never keeps out the wet?
A   The roof of your mouth!

Q   If teacher sits on a drawing
     pin, what time of the
     year will it foretell?
A   An early spring!

Q   What word is always pronounced wrongly?
A   Wrongly!

Q   Which is the worst month for soldiers?
A   A long March!

Q   What is there in your house that ought to be looked
     into?
A   A mirror!

Q   What is the easiest way to double your money?
A   Fold it!

Q   What sort of necktie would a pig wear?
A   A pig's tie (pigsty)!

Q   Why should Ireland be the richest country in the
     world?
A   Because its capital is always Dublin (doubling)!

Q   What is the best thing to put in a pie?
A   Your teeth!

Q   Why is the rain different from Sunday?
A   Because it can fall on any day of the week!

Q   Why is your nose in the middle of your face?
A   Because it is the scenter (centre)!

Q   Why does a Red Indian wear feathers in his hair?
A   To keep his wig warm (wigwam)!

Q   Why is tennis a noisy game?
A   Because each player raises a racket!

Q   Why should a coal dealer never lose his stock?
A   Because it always goes to the cellar (seller)!

Q   Why is it always cool in a sports arena?
A   Because there are hundreds of fans in the seats!

Q   Which is correct, the yolk of an egg *is* white, or the yolk of an egg *are* white?
A   The yolk of an egg is yellow!

Q   Which is better, complete happiness or a crust of bread?
A   A crust of bread. Nothing is better than complete happiness, but a crust of bread is better than nothing!

Q   Which candle burns longer, a white candle or a red candle?
A   Neither. They both burn shorter!

Q   Which spider has most legs, one spider or no spider?
A   No spider has ten legs and that is more than any other spider has!

Q   Which is heavier, the full moon or half a moon?
A   Half a moon because a full moon is twice as light as half a moon!

Q   Which of your relatives depend on you for their
    very existence?
A   Your uncles, aunts, cousins. Because without U they
    could not exist!

Q   When is a pretty girl like a boat?
A   When she's attached to a boy (buoy)!

Q   What did the cloud say to the sun?
A   'I've got you covered!'

Q   Which three girls are always unlucky?
A   Miss Hap, Miss Fortune and Miss Chance!

Q   Where was Queen Victoria crowned?
A   On the head!

Q   Where will you always find gold?
A   In the dictionary!

Q   What is the hardest thing about helping someone
    to catch a train?
A   Throwing it to them!

Q   If a pen and a writing pad had a race, which would
    win?
A   The pen. The writing pad would remain stationary
    (stationery)!

Q   If there were ten crows in a tree and you shot one,
    how many would remain?
A   None. The rest would fly away!

Q   If you threw a stone at a rooster, what would it say?
A   I can't repeat it. It was foul (fowl) language!

Q If bread is a loaf in London, what are windows in Birmingham?
A Glass!

Q If a two-wheeled conveyance is a bicycle and a three-wheeled conveyance is a tricycle, what is a five-wheeled conveyance?
A A vehicle (V-hicle)!

Q What must a person be sure to do before giving first-aid?
A Wait till there's an accident!

Q What did the big shoe say to the little shoe?
A 'You'll do in a pinch!'

Q Why is a churn like a caterpillar?
A Because it makes the butterfly (butter fly)!

Q Why is a skunk the most generous animal in the world?
A Because it will give a cent (scent) to its worst enemy!

Q Why is a nut like a regiment?
A Because it has a kernel (colonel)!

Q Why is a gardener better paid than a carpenter?
A Because he has the most salary (celery)!

Q When is an apple not an apple?
A When it's a crab!

Q Why is a broken window like a toothache?
A Because it's a bad pane (pain)!

Q   Why is a bride like a railway?
A   Because she has a train!

Q   Where does the carpenter strike the first nail when
    he builds a house?
A   On the head!

Q   When is a good umbrella like an old, worn
    umbrella?
A   When it is used up!

Q   What coat has no sleeves?
A   It could be a waistcoat but it could also be a coat of
    paint!

Q   What is hot when it is cold?
A   Mustard!

Q   What has no legs but runs when it is warm?
A   Butter!

Q   What is full of holes but holds water?
A   A sponge!

Q   What table has no legs?
A   A time-table!

Q   What bell never rings?
A   A bluebell!

Q   Which is the brightest day?
A   Sunday (Sun-day)!

Q   When is an engine like an artist?
A   When it draws a train!

Q Who can jump higher than an apple tree?
A An apple tree cannot jump!

Q Which moves faster, heat or cold?
A Heat, because it is very easy to catch a cold!

Q If there were only three girls in the world what would they talk about?
A Two would get together and talk about the third!

Q Where do you go when you are fourteen?
A Into your fifteenth year!

Q Where can you always find money?
A In the dictionary!

Q Where is the best place to get fat?
A In a butcher's shop!

Q If a burglar got into the coal cellar, would the coal shoot? (chute)!
A No, but the fire would (wood)!

Q If a man had a packet of cigarettes but no matches, how would he have a smoke?
A He would take a cigarette out of the packet and it would then be a cigarette lighter!

Q Which window in a house is like the moon?
A The sky light!

A zoo full of riddles

Q What animal sounds as though it had a sore throat?
A A horse (hoarse)!

Q What animals would you find in a bank?
A Bucks and doe (dough)!

Q What animal would you find on a legal document?
A A seal!

Q What animal plays cricket?
A A bat!

Q What animal goes naked?
A A bear (bare)!

Q What animal do you carry
   on the top of your head?
A The hare (hair)!

Q What animal directs your bicycle?
A A steer!

Q What animal is tiresome?
A A boar (bore)!

Q What animal can we spell with one letter?
A U! (you)!

Q What two animals walk with you wherever you go?
A Calves!

Q What animal is a cannibal?
A A cow because it eats fodder (father)!

Q Which is the heaviest animal?
A A led (lead) horse!

Q Which animal would you like to meet in the desert, darling?
A Reindeer (rain, dear)!

Q What animal gets suddenly quiet?
A The dingo (din go)!

Q When can you spell the King of Beasts with one letter?
A When he's a 'C' lion (sea lion)!

Q What insect is a popular summer game?
A The cricket!

Q Which animal do you find starting most letters?
A The deer (Dear Sir,)!

Q Why did the zebra complain of seeing spots before its eyes?
A He was married to a leopard!

Q How can you tell if an elephant has been in the fridge?
A By the footprints in the butter!

Q Why do elephants have wrinkled knees?
A From playing marbles!

Q   Why do elephants have flat feet?
A   From jumping over palm trees!

Q   What do elephants have that no other animal has?
A   Baby elephants!

Q   What is the difference between a white elephant and a lemon?
A   The lemon is yellow!

Q   What animal do we associate with Lady Godiva?
A   The bear (bare)!

Q   When is a bee sting like a piece of material?
A   When it is felt!

Q   Why is a horse a most unusual feeder?
A   It eats best when there isn't a bit in its mouth!

Q   Why does tying a slow horse to a fence make it a better racer?
A   It makes it fast!

Q   If a man gets up on a donkey, what does he get down from?
A   An eider duck!

Q   Why is a dog biting its tail like a good housewife?
A   Because it is making both ends meet!

Q   Why is a cat longer at night than it is in the morning?
A   Because it is let out at night and taken in in the morning!

Q Why is a hill like a lazy dog?
A Because a hill is an inclined plane; an inclined plane is a slope up and a slow pup is a lazy dog!

Q Why is a sick pig such an unusual animal?
A Because it must be killed before it can be cured!

Q Which would you rather have, a lion to eat you or a tiger?
A I would rather have the lion eat the tiger!

Q What fish would you find in a hen roost?
A A perch!

Q What animal has its eyes closest together?
A The smallest animal!

Q What part of a fish weighs the most?
A The scales!

My sister Kate

Questions

1. What is the word when my sister Kate passes on news to her friend?
2. What is the word when my sister Kate leaves home?
3. What is the word when my sister Kate looks after the house?
4. What is the word when my sister Kate can't breathe?
5. What is the word when my sister Kate gets two similar presents for her birthday?
6. What is the word when my sister Kate chews her food?
7. What is the word when my sister Kate makes a prophecy?
8. What is the word when my sister Kate does to others as they do to her?
9. What is the word when my sister Kate makes a dress?
10. What is the word when my sister Kate gets a document to say she has done well at school?

Answers

1. Communicate
2. Vacate
3. Domesticate
4. Suffocate
5. Duplicate
6. Masticate
7. Prognosticate
8. Reciprocate
9. Fabricate
10. Certificate

The cat with nine lives

Questions
1 When did the cat look like a worm?
2 When did the cat look like a waterfall?
3 When did the cat look like a list?
4 When did the cat become a quiz cat?
5 When did the cat become a church cat?
6 When did the cat become a sailing boat?
7 When did the cat become a shooting cat?
8 When did the cat become a tragedy?
9 When did the cat become a farmer's cat?

Answers
1 When it became a caterpillar
2 When it became a cateract
3 When it became a catalogue
4 When it became a catechism
5 When it became a cathedral
6 When it becomes a catamaran
7 When it became a catapult
8 When it became a catastrophe
9 When it became cattle

Riddles in rhyme

Some of these riddles are very old. Where I have been able to trace it, I have given the date when the riddle was first printed.

> As I was going to St Ives,
> I met a man who had seven wives.
> Each wife had seven sacks,
> Each sack had seven cats,
> Each cat had seven kits.
> Kits, cats, sacks and wives,
> How many were going to St Ives?   (1730)

Answer: One. All the others were coming *from* St Ives.

> Two legs sat upon three legs
> with one leg in his lap.
> In comes four legs
> and runs away with one leg.
> Up jumps two legs,
> Catches up three legs,
> Throws it after four legs
> And makes him bring back one leg.   (1600)

Answer: A man is sitting on a stool eating a leg of mutton. A dog grabs the leg of mutton and runs off with it. The man jumps up and throws his stool at the dog. The dog brings back the leg of mutton.

> Little Nancy Etticoat,
> With a white petticoat
> And a red nose.
> She has no feet or hands,
> But the longer she stands
> The shorter she grows.   (1645)

Answer: A candle.

Round like an apple,
Deep like a cup,
All the King's horses
Can't pull it up. (1645)

Answer: A well.

Thirty white horses
Upon a red hill.
They tramp, tramp, tramp.
They champ, champ, champ.
Then they stand still. (17th century)

Answer: The teeth and gums.

Two and Thirty white Bulls
Standing in a stall,
Out came the red Bull
And licked them all.

Answer: The teeth and tongue.

I am black and much admired,
Many seek me till they're tired;
I weary horse and I weary man.
Solve this riddle if you can. (1817)

Answer: Coal.

Two brothers we are, great burdens we bear
By which we are heavily pressed;
The truth is to say, we are full all the day,
And empty when we go to rest. (1600)

Answer: A pair of shoes.

What God never sees,
What the King seldom sees,
What we see every day.
Read my riddle, I pray. (1505)

Answer: An equal.

Marble walls as white as milk,
A dainty lining, soft as silk;
Within a pool crystal-clear,
A golden apple doth appear.
No doors there are in this stronghold,
　Yet thieves break in and steal the gold.　(1810)
Answer: An egg.

There's three of us in six, there's five of us in seven,
　There's four of us in nine, and six are in eleven.
Answer: Letters.

The mother of men was a lady whose name
　Read forward or backward is always the same.
Answer: Eve.

Flour of England, fruit of Spain,
Came together in a shower of rain;
Put in a bag, tied round with a string;
If you'll tell me this riddle
I'll give you a ring.
Answer: A plum pudding.
(This rhyme was known in the time of Queen Mary and
some people think that it describes the meeting of the
Queen with King Philip of Spain which took place in
'downpouring rain'. Mary publicly sent Philip a ring
to symbolise their marriage. And the last line might
be a reference to that.)

Perhaps the best-known riddle in rhyme is Humpty
Dumpty.

> Humpty Dumpty sat on a wall,
> Humpty Dumpty had a great fall.
> All the king's horses and all the king's men,
> Couldn't put Humpty together again.

Answer: An egg.

And last of all in this book are two very old riddles.
I have included them because no one has ever been able
to find a satisfactory answer to either of them. Perhaps
you can. This is the first one:

> Twelve pears hanging high,
> Twelve knights riding by;
> Each knight took a pear
> And left eleven hanging there.

The only answer *I* can think of is that 'Each knight'
was the name of the knight who took the pear!

This is the other riddle which has puzzled people for
more than three hundred and fifty years:

> The fiddler and his wife,
> The piper and his mother
> Ate three half cakes, three whole cakes
> And three-quarters of another.

What I think it means is that each person ate one whole
cake, one half a cake and one quarter of a cake, which
would imply that there were only three people, in which
case the fiddler's wife was the piper's mother.

What do you think?